LETTS HOME DECORATOR

LIGHTING

JILL BLAKE

NEW HOLLAND

First published in the UK in 1995 by
New Holland (Publishers) Ltd
Chapel House, 24 Nutford Place
London W1H 6DQ

ISBN 1 85238 538 3

Designed and edited by
Anness Publishing Ltd
Boundary Row Studios
1 Boundary Row
London SE1 8HP

Editorial Director: Joanna Lorenz
Project Editor: Lindsay Porter
Design: Millions Design
Special photography: John Freeman
Illustrations: King & King Associates

Printed and bound in Singapore
by Tien Wah Press (Pte) Ltd

CONTENTS

INTRODUCTION

Lighting is so frequently overlooked when planning a home, yet it is essential to the successful running of every house and work space. If planned carefully, right from the beginning, well-thought out lighting can create an attractive and comfortable home, practical work areas or happy playing space.

Proper planning, before the colour scheme is chosen and the decorating is done, is vital if you want to achieve a successful result. If lighting is thought of simply as an accessory or after-thought, it will be far too late to cut holes in ceilings or channel out walls to install cables and fittings. Lighting needs to be readily available at the flip of a switch – exactly where and when you want it.

Good lighting can set the mood of a room, making it tranquil and restful or warm and lively. It can visually correct bad proportions in a room, such as a high ceiling or a narrow hallway. And, of course, lighting is essential for reading, working at a computer or even watching television without straining your eyes or back.

Lighting may be decorative, but it also serves a vital purpose and this book will take you through all the elements of planning and selecting your lighting scheme within the limits of your budget.

Below: *Work areas must be well lit. The desk is practically sited near the window during the day. At night, the desk lamp – easily portable – can be used on the desk for close work, or placed on the display shelves when the wheeled trolley is being used for other purposes.*

BEGIN AT THE BEGINNING

Once you have decided how you are going to use your rooms, and have some idea of what you want to accommodate in the way of people, furniture and appliances, you will need to make some scale plans (*see* pages 8–9), even possibly models, to work out exactly how you are going to fit everything in, and to help you to relate the power and lighting to the position of the furniture and other equipment.

With lighting, it can be difficult to judge the visual effect of your ideas in plan form. One practical way of assessing how directional light will fall in a room is to arm yourself with a kit rather like the one used by car repair shops to see inside (and under) the engines of cars – a naked bulb in a wire 'cage' on a long flex. This will help you with positions for lighting fittings. Get a friend to help by holding the light while you review the various effects it creates and be sure to use a long well-insulated lead and make sure any connections are safe.

KNOW YOUR LIMITATIONS

When you have established a 'master plan', and have decided where you want to position furniture and light fittings, you may need to call in a qualified electrician or other expert. Ask them for advice and estimates of the time a job will take as well as the cost – it is always wise to have two or three different costings for each job. And make sure the tradesman is an approved contractor (particularly important with electricians).

Unless you are a qualified electrician, you should call in the expert to do any complicated rewiring; install ceiling and wall fittings; add extra power points and sockets; or alter switching circuits. You

Above: *Bookshelves in a study are spotlit from above so the titles can be read easily. The spots also provide illumination for the desk area.*

should also seek their help if you are going to light the garden extensively – especially if the lighting is to be combined with water for an ornamental garden or swimming pool. You may be able to install simple fittings in the garden yourself, but always make sure that any cable used is the special heavy-duty exterior type – either MICC (metal-insulated copper-clad cable) or twin-cored armoured cable – and is properly earthed. In many cases it may have to be embedded in the ground.

Whether you plan to cope with a simple job yourself, or plan to call in an electrician, you need to work out exactly what your requirements are, so you can discuss them fully at the outset. This is why the first section of the book is devoted to the practical aspects of planning. The positioning of furniture, equipment and appliances should be plotted accurately, so the placing of light fittings will relate, and will illuminate the required surfaces clearly, but without glare or dazzle. When it is mapped out, you can show your proposed plan to the expert, or the lighting supplier, and work out exactly what fittings to use where.

LIGHTING DESIGN

If you have a complicated lighting problem you may prefer to ask a professional lighting designer for help – they will work with you; draw up a lighting plan (see page 9) and work out what fittings to use. They will also work within an agreed budget, so this might not be as expensive as you might suspect, and could, in fact, save you from making a costly mistake. Electrical and lighting suppliers may have their own design departments, or may be able to recommend a good freelance designer, otherwise a qualified local interior designer could probably advise you.

The aim of this book is to introduce you to the possibilities, to help you assess your surroundings and requirements and guide you through the planning and conception of different lighting schemes so that you achieve the very best results.

Above: *Display shelves look twice as exciting when they are well lit, and will create a welcoming background glow in almost any room. Here, shelves in a recess in a dining area are* lit from spots above, and an uplighter from below, to throw the floral display into strong relief, and enhance the fruit bowl.

PLANNING AND MEASURING UP

Electric power is one of the essential services which you have to consider when designing a room or living space. Just as you need to have water 'on tap' in the right place to supply sinks, baths, basins, and lavatories, so you require your electricity and lighting to be in the correct place to provide power, and to illuminate surfaces according to the function of the room.

Yet lighting still tends to be treated as an accessory, and is often added at the end of the planning and decorating process, when in fact it should be one of the tasks which is tackled at the outset – at the basic planning stage. Lighting may be decorative – but it should be an integral part of the scheme. It will help you to create mood; it can also help you to create 'visual tricks', seemingly adjusting the proportions of a room.

Above: *In a sophisticated setting the eye is carried through from area to area, creating an impression of space. Downlighters are recessed in the ceiling to provide background lighting; wall-washers light the wallhangings; other portable fittings are on a separate circuit.*

COLOUR AND LIGHT

Sensations of colour do not exist without light and, scientifically speaking, the colour of an object results from the selective absorption of light energy by its atoms. The eye sees an object only by the light it reflects, so the wavelengths it reflects determine its colour. Some objects reflect and absorb light of all different wavelengths equally well – white snow reflects nearly all the incidental light, so it looks bright and shiny; black velvet absorbs nearly all the light that falls on it, so it looks dark and dull. Coloured objects are capable of selective absorption, which is why we see them as coloured – and the *type* of light used can appear to change their colour. Most people consider a clear daylight to give the truest colour rendition, but this is not necessarily so, since strong sunlight, for example, can give a yellowish cast.

All surfaces have a texture, and the way light actually strikes the surface can make colour look different too. Red, for example, on a shiny surface will look much stronger and brighter than it does on a matt, light-absorbing one, even though the same pigment or dyes have been used.

But it is after dark that the differences can be seen much more strongly. In some cases a colour appears to change completely when it is viewed under night (artificial) lighting – so much so that a colour scheme which looks perfectly acceptable in the daytime may appear mis-matched under artificial light. Although most colours are affected to some degree, some of the yellow-greens (olive greens for example) absorb so much light they can look almost black under artificial lighting. This is why it is essential to see colour

Right and below: *Lighting in the living-room should be flexible – and help to create ambience. The different pastel-coloured bulbs change the mood from warm to cool and restful. The different wall lights – traditional wall sconces or wall-mounted uplighters – also change the effect.*

samples under both day and night lighting conditions in the actual room where they will be used, before a final decision is reached. This means that in an ideal world the actual light fittings would be installed before choosing colours and selecting fabrics, wallcoverings, floorings etc. Unfortunately this is rarely possible.

Some modern light fittings such as low-voltage tungsten-halogen bulbs (called *lamps*) provide a much finer white light than the normal mains voltage incandescent light bulb, and improve colour rendition, but may not necessarily be suitable for your domestic lighting plan. All too often, a light fitting is bought not for the effect and quality of light which it will give, but as a piece of decoration in its own right.

Although you obviously want a fitting to be aesthetically pleasing, it also has to be functional – you would not choose a cooker, washing machine, dishwasher or other domestic appliance on looks alone; nor would you choose a chair or sofa without sitting on it; or a bed without lying down on it.

LOOKING AT LIGHTS

There are also problems with 'visualizing' lighting – a light fitting viewed in a showroom or shop (just as with small colour samples of paint, flooring, wallcovering and fabric) cannot really be judged until it is brought home, installed and *lit*. This way you can judge the quality and amount of light it gives

out. But also consider a fitting unlit, as it will be seen during the daytime as a passive part of the decorating scheme. Coloured shades, in particular, can take on quite a different look and colour when the light is shining on them during the day, as opposed to when they are lit at night.

PROFESSIONAL HELP

As lighting is such a specialized subject, and such a highly visual one, which cannot really be demonstrated in illustrations, nor effectively described in words, you really do need to see actual fittings for yourself. Don't be afraid to ask for help and advice: most lighting departments in stores, and specialist lighting shops are aware of the various aspects of lighting. Assistants should have been trained to be helpful – if not, go elsewhere.

It is also possible to visit the showrooms of some major lighting manufacturers, where you can 'play' with the fittings. And if there are some aspects you are unsure about, don't be afraid or embarrassed to call in expert help. It may be wise to ask a professional lighting designer to work with you on a very complex job.

But before you get this far, you need to plan the purpose and function of each room, and decide exactly where you are going to position the furniture and appliances so you can relate the light and power sources to this master plan.

Below and bottom: *Bedroom lighting must be flexible as these two areas of one room show. In the sleeping area the bed has subtle lighting concealed underneath the canopy, and uplighters illuminating the bedside tables. In the dressing area the mirror and dressing table have strip lighting concealed behind a baffle.*

PRACTICAL PLANNING

'Get it right' on paper first, by making floor plans to scale of each room. Plans of walls are called elevations, and you may need to make these too, when it comes to fitting in your lighting. Also make an overall floor plan showing how the various rooms relate to each other and to the hall, stair and landing area. This master plan will enable you to cope with any structural alterations at the outset – installation of cables, or cutting holes in walls and ceilings to accommodate electrical fittings are classed as structural jobs.

Measure up accurately using a steel rule or tape (fabric ones stretch in use), allowing for projections and recesses, and existing built-in items. It is useful to have a helper to hold the end of the tape and to double-check your arithmetic – make sure you measure on the true vertical and horizontal using a plumb line or spirit level to check.

Plot positions of electrical points, socket outlets and plumbing pipes. Don't forget to 'think three-dimensionally' and measure the depth and height of skirting boards (baseboards), dados (chair rails) and cornices; the height of window sills from the floor; the depth and width of sills, window frames, reveals and architraves since such projections may have to be accommodated when you are planning furniture positions and relating lighting to these.

Draw out the plan to scale on either plain or squared paper – the most common scales are 1:50, 1:25 and 1:20 (1 metre of room space to 50, 25 or 20 mm) or 1 foot of room space to ½-inch on the plan. Use a set square and ruler to ensure straight lines.

Make templates in the same scale as the floor plan, of all the items of furniture, bathroom or kitchen equipment you intend to put into the room – allow for existing items as well as any proposed purchases. It helps to colour them, so they can be seen on the plan more easily. You could use a colour code if necessary, with one colour for old items, another for new, and a third for 'possibles'. You can buy special architects' transparent templates, in various scales, from graphic design and artists' supply shops to make the task easier – just trace through the shape onto plain card or paper and cut out. Do remember to buy the same scale of furniture template as the floor plan.

Move the cut-out shapes about on the plan until you reach a satisfactory arrangement. You can draw in the furniture positions on

your final plan, but always work with templates first. Remember to allow for the opening of doors and drawers; pushing chairs back from tables; moving around furniture; crossing the room – this is called the 'traffic flow' (see diagram below).

Once these positions are established, you can plan lighting, plumbing and power supplies so they are sited exactly where they are needed. Lighting can be centrally positioned over a dining-table for example, or planned to illuminate clearly a desk, hobby bench or work surfaces in the kitchen, without glare or shadow; power supplies can be provided for appliances and equipment – TV, video, computer terminal, music centres etc – exactly where required.

Below: Plotting your room on graph paper ensures you will get it right from the start. Draw out the plan of your room to scale, and cut out furniture to the same scale. Position the furniture on the floor plan until you have achieved a pleasing and practical arrangement.

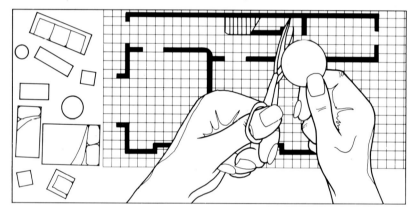

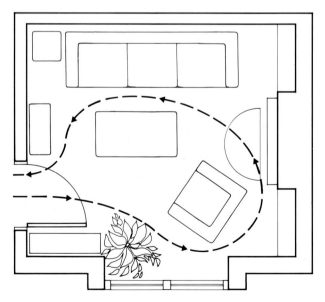

Above: Don't forget to allow for movement around the room – plan for access to storage facilities, sockets, opening of doors, drawers and windows. This is known as the 'traffic flow'.

PLAN AHEAD

If you are only dealing with one area at a time, but there is a whole house or apartment to do room by room, plan all the rooms – their purpose and function, eventual furniture positions and structural alterations – at the start. This way you can get the electrics and lighting, plumbing and building work and joinery done all at the outset. This will be cheaper in the long run than if you keep calling back the various tradesmen each time you can afford to do a room.

MAKING A LIGHTING PLAN

Once you have your basic floor plan, and know exactly where you are going to position the furniture, you will need to relate it to a lighting plan. An easy way to do this is by using an overlay of tissue paper or transparent acetate sheeting (available from graphic design suppliers). Trace the outline of the room shape, marking in position of doors and windows.

Draw in the positions of the proposed light fittings, so they come exactly where you want them in relation to the appliances and furniture – a light over the exact centre of the dining-table for example. Use a different colour for each circuit (red for power, blue for background and general lighting, green for task/lamps etc), and trace back to the switching point (*see* diagram below).

Because the floor plan is in scale, the lighting plan will also be in scale, and an electrician should be able to position the fittings following this. If necessary, you may have to draw elevations of the walls to show positions of wall lights and other wall-mounted fittings. If you are planning any off-centre positions for fittings (like downlighters in the ceiling) make sure you explain to the electrician exactly what you are doing, and why you want the fittings in unusual places.

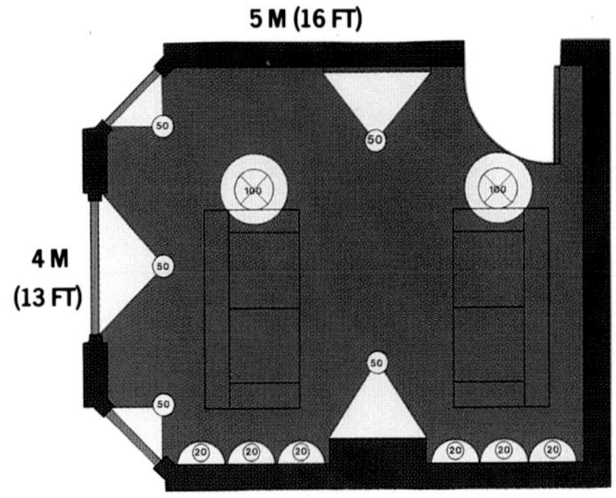

LIVING-ROOM

5 M × 4 M = 20 SQ METRES
(16 FT × 13 FT = 208 SQ FEET)

6 × 20 W = 120 WATTS
5 × 50 W = 250 WATTS
2 × 100 W = 200 WATTS

Above: *An example of a professional lighting plan. The dimensions of the room, plus furniture, doors and windows are positioned to scale, with the wattage of the light sources included. The total wattage will be divided by the surface of the room to determine the average wattage per square metre (foot).*

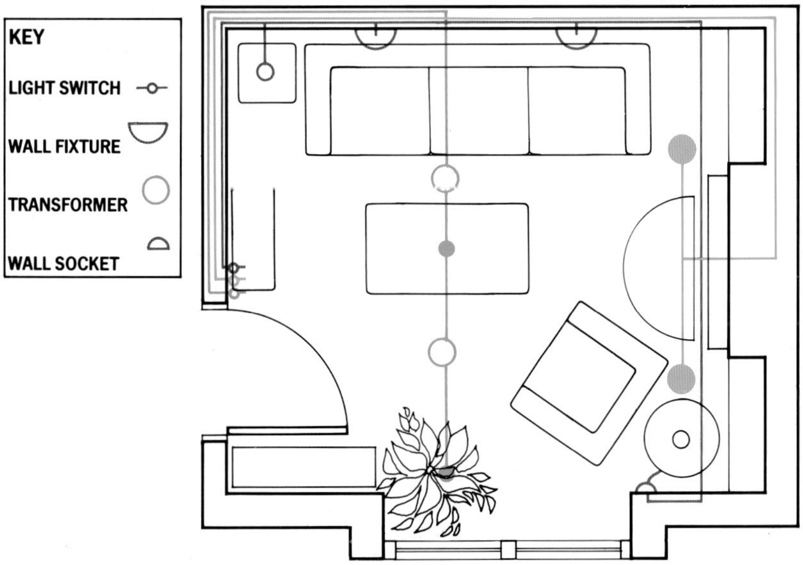

Left: *This room incorporates three lighting circuits. The red circuit operates the wall sconces, table lamp and standard lamp. The blue circuit operates two recessed downlighters which illuminate the book shelves, and provide background lighting. The green circuit operates the low-voltage fixtures, the recessed spotlight used to accent the plant, and the downlighter illuminating objects on the coffee table. The mood can be changed at the flick of a switch.*

CHECKLIST FOR PLANNING
A LIGHTING SCHEME

Practicalities
Look at structure – can walls be channelled to take fittings; can fittings be recessed into the ceiling (if so what is the depth); is there access to the ceiling from above; are there any restrictions on the installation of new wiring?

Space and mood
Assess space to be lit – how is it to be used; does it need 'correcting' visually; what type of ambience is most important – or must this be flexible?

Design
What type of colour scheme is proposed; what are the main items of furniture, and where will they be positioned; what textures and surface treatments will be used on floors, walls and windows?

Features for highlighting
Are these architectural – cornices, niches, columns, etc; or decorative – paintings, wallhangings, sculpture, furniture, or plants?

Control
How many circuits and which ones need to be dimmable; where should switches be positioned; should any fittings be dual-switched (eg hall/landing area)?

DESIGN DECISIONS

Once you have prepared scale plans and decided where the furniture and the fittings will be positioned, you will have to reach some design decisions – and work out exactly what you need to illuminate. You will also need to relate the various different types of lighting – task, general or background, and accent or display lighting – to your master plan.

First of all, try to relate the space to the atmosphere you want to create. By all means think of the purpose of the room and how it is to be used, but also decide on the *mood* which you want it to have. Consider the main features to be highlighted and plot light sources accordingly. Consider what might be better unlit, or specifically illuminated so it throws a shadow onto another surface, or helps to take the eye into another area or

room – and so appears to increase the overall space.

You will also need to think about practical aspects: are there likely to be any restrictions on the installation of new wiring, such as no access from above or a concrete wall or ceiling which cannot be channelled out to take fittings? Where is the best place to site controls; which lights should be dual-switched; how many circuits should there be? In large or dual-purpose rooms you will want the lighting to be as flexible as possible, allowing one area to be dimmed while the other end is being used and lit, so several circuits are essential. You should also consider how many of the circuits should be on dimmer switches and how much of the lighting is to be invisible and how much is to be more of an accessory, contributing to the theme of the room.

Right: *Flexible lighting in a sophisticated living-room adds drama to the dark-coloured walls. Table lamps provide pools of intimate light; wall-mounted sconces throw light up onto the ceiling and illuminate the wall; the central chandelier can be turned on for extra brilliance; and uplighters are strategically positioned in the room. These are all on different circuits and some are dimmer controlled.*

STYLED TO SUIT

Conflict of architectural style can sometimes present problems – a traditional property simply does not look right equipped with large, shiny modern light fittings. Unobtrusive fittings, such as cleverly concealed spotlights, downlighters and uplighters can work wonders, however, and low-voltage lighting works particularly well in situations where you want the light source to be subtle, but the level of light to be fairly strong.

Period wall panelling would be totally spoilt if it was festooned with large light fittings. Decorative ceiling mouldings and cornices should be emphasized, and preferably lit from below. Vast holes should not be cut in such ceilings, nor should aggressive pendant fittings detract from them. It is sometimes possible to install discreet recessed downlighters – the low-voltage types are smaller and neater.

If a decorative ceiling exists in a room used as a kitchen or bathroom, don't spoil it with ugly fluorescent fittings. Spotlighting on track can sometimes be acceptable in such a situation as long as the lights themselves on the track are not too bulky. Paint the track to match the ceiling colour to keep it from dominating the room.

An art deco room often relies on fittings of the period to enhance the style – the beautiful shell-shaped and Egyptian-inspired wall lights; the glass pendants suspended on chains; lamps with graceful female figures bearing the light as a globe or flower; or streamlined, elongated bathroom and dressing-table lights, often wall-mounted to the side of the mirror. Lamps based on

Above: *Black-lacquered metal pendant lamps on rise-and-fall fittings light the dining area in a modern kitchen in bleached maple.*

original designs of the period are still being made and modern interpretations of these styles are also readily available.

Tiffany-style table lamps and pendants are available from many lighting shops. These are no longer ridiculously expensive and usually incorporate attractively coloured glass which can throw decorative patterns onto a wall, ceiling or surrounding area, and will add to the charm of a turn-of-the-century ambience.

Many modern minimalist or hi-tech interiors also rely on light fittings to help create the style – spotlight on track, streamlined swan-necked uplighters or industrial fittings from hospital and office furniture catalogues will echo the pared-down theme.

The country cottage or farmhouse may need simple and cosy lighting, mainly from lamps, cleverly positioned ceiling pendants

and wall lights, but other lighting can be provided from downlighters, uplighters and spots, as long as they are not too aggressive and don't overwhelm the basic style.

FITTINGS AND WALL HEIGHT

On a practical note, rooms in old or country-style houses in particular are frequently low-ceilinged. If wall lights of the conventional 'olde worlde' type (which usually take candle bulbs) are fixed too high up, they will scorch the ceiling. Bulbs should be of suitably low wattage in this situation too, and there are some fittings available which can be covered to prevent discoloration. Alternatively, use a wider-angled light source. Pendant fittings are rarely suitable in low-ceilinged rooms – people will literally walk into them. In many cases, uplighters or wall-washers are a better choice as they will make a low ceiling seem higher (*see* Tricks of the Light).

Wall lights need to be positioned correctly in a tall room. Placed too high up, they don't serve any useful purpose and if too low they will emphasize the height of the room. This might be the moment to draw some plans with wall elevations to work out their exact position (*see* Planning and Measuring Up). Pendant fittings and chandeliers also come into their own in this situation, with an opportunity for some interesting and dramatic means of suspension.

Right: *Spotlights are concealed behind the beams in a country-style setting, and can be angled towards worktops, cooker and sink.*

When it finally comes down to making a lighting design decision, the actual purpose and function of the room generally dictates the type of lighting required and to some extent the choice of fitting. So start at the beginning – by the front door (for porch and exterior lighting *see* pages 38–43) and then come into the hall.

HALL, STAIRS AND LANDING

This area of the home needs good overall lighting to provide a warm welcome without glare. The stairs should be clearly lit to prevent accidents and the landing should also be well lit. If there are young children in the home who are afraid of the dark, the landing light level might be controlled by a dimmer switch, so a soft light can be left on all night. Some of these can be programmed to switch off at a certain time. The lighting in this area usually needs to be dual-switched so it can be controlled from the front door, or hall and landing.

A pendant light on the landing, and one or two in the hall may be sufficient in a small house, although in a larger one you might prefer to use a glittering chandelier in the hall. Alternatively use wall-washers to light

one wall (perhaps the one at the side of the stairs). Downlighters strategically positioned in the ceiling may provide sufficient background glow. Wall lights or wall-mounted uplighters can help to add height and make a narrow area look wider, but avoid 'stepping' the fittings up the stair wall and make sure the bulbs do not cause glare when descending the staircase, so avoid the linear tungsten halogen type unless the fittings can be placed high enough up.

Sometimes a hall is long and narrow, or is nothing more than a dark tunnel. To light this successfully, try to include multiple fittings and some points of interest which can be lit dramatically. Groups of recessed downlighters, or spots on track lighting walls alternately to the left and right can work wonders in a bleak corridor or hall. Some accent lighting will also create interest. Choose the method of accenting to suit the item to be lit – a hall table (where you may need to illuminate a mirror), a picture or collection of prints, an attractive rug or other interesting flooring or a group of plants – and to correspond with the architectural style of the property. Visible light fixtures should not be at odds with the decor.

Above: A large hall in classical style has ceiling-recessed downlighters positioned to light the curving stairwell, emphasize the cornice and highlight flowers and the telephone on the storage unit.

Above: *Hall lighting in a modern apartment where the ceiling is somebody else's floor. A special 'box' was constructed over the existing power outlet to take four recessed low-voltage downlighters to provide general lighting and illuminate the decorative rug on the stripped floorboards; two directional fittings light the picture.*

KITCHENS

The kitchen is the main 'work room' in the house, but is often a dual-purpose area which has to incorporate accurate task lighting around the cooker, work surfaces, and the sink. The sink may be positioned under a window, where during the day it will be well lit, but adequate night illumination is often forgotten, and you may find yourself working in your own shadow.

As kitchens also tend to be used as dining areas – even if only for a snack at the breakfast bar – this will require specific illumination, separately switched so the table can be lit when the rest of the room is dimmed or dark. There may also be a need for display lighting in an alcove, cupboard or directed towards a dresser.

Above: *A pendant with naked bulb will shine into the eyes.*

Above: *A pendant on a rise-and-fall fitting will prevent glare.*

Above: *Deep cupboards will need some form of lighting. Conceal fittings above.*

Below: *Strategically positioned downlighters around the perimeter of the ceiling light work surfaces; four are positioned over the central food preparation island, and don't detract from the traditional atmosphere in this hand-crafted country-style kitchen.*

One of the tried-and-tested ways of lighting work surfaces is by fitting tubular lighting under a wall-mounted cupboard above the units, with a baffle or diffusing reflector in front so the light shines onto the surface without dazzling the person preparing the food. But there is no reason why you should not use downlighters, spots, or even a series of pendant lights. These are all practical when there is no top cupboard to cast a shadow on the surface.

If the cooker does not have a hood over it with integral light illuminating the top, the possibilities mentioned above may be suitable. One interesting way of giving a good overall diffused light, if the kitchen is tall enough, is to mount fluorescent tubes *above* the wall cupboards and conceal them with a wooden batten. However, there must be about 75 cm (30 inches) of space between the tube and the ceiling.

Long fluorescent tubes have been popular for kitchen lighting for many years, but the light is flat, bright and usually unattractive. A 'warmer' tube can be used (*see* the chart opposite) which will improve the atmosphere, but check the effect it will have on the food. A very pinkish cast will cause meat to look undercooked.

For a really 'sparkly' even light in the kitchen, 'starlights' can be used. These are tiny low-voltage fittings which create a magical effect. Lighting track with spots along the length is a popular light fitting for kitchens, since it can be fixed into an existing socket and incorporates several spotlights which can be angled towards various surfaces. In some kitchens two or three may be necessary. This type of lighting can be positioned over the sink or work surface, or

Colour Effects of Fluorescent Tubes		
Tube	**Colour effect**	**Purpose**
Daylight (Cool white)	cool	general lighting; blends with daylight
De luxe natural (De luxe white)	warm	general lighting; for food stores
Kolor-ite (De luxe warm white)	intermediate	general lighting; best colour rendition
Natural	intermediate	general lighting
Northlight (Colour-matching)	cool	for matching materials
Plus-white	intermediate	general lighting
Warm white	warm	general lighting
White	intermediate	general lighting; very efficient

Above: *Three ceiling-recessed downlighters light an often forgotten area – the sink – in this brightly coloured, modernist kitchen.*

over the table and combined with ceiling-recessed downlighters in the rest of the room.

In the dining area, the light needs to be centrally positioned over the dining-table. This can be done by a pendant on a rise-and-fall fitting, or by strategically positioned downlighters, which, if the table is large, may mean setting four into the ceiling, arranged so the beams cross at table point. Wire this lighting on a separate circuit so the rest of the kitchen can be in darkness when eating.

Again, aim for the style of the lighting to suit the style of the room. The more modern streamlined kitchen can take gleaming chrome and steel fittings; curved 'trunking'-type lighting which can be suspended above a centre island unit or work area; sophisticated spots and fluorescents. The country-style kitchen will need softer lighting and more traditional or unobtrusive fittings.

Don't forget the insides of kitchen cupboards, larders and pantries – these may need to be illuminated, especially if they are

deep. A light fitting which is controlled from a switch on the door jamb is the most practical, but an awkward corner can be lit by a spot, which will illuminate the inside of the cupboard at the same time.

WORK ROOMS

A work room may be a study or 'home office', the garage or hobby area. Most of the kitchen lighting principles can also be applied to work rooms, although the whole room may need a higher degree of overall lighting in order for the various tasks to be performed in comfort. This might be provided by downlighters, uplighters or wall-washers, but a certain amount of task lighting will also be necessary – flexible, adjustable desk lamps for typing and computer work; a large 'studio-size' anglepoise might be used as an uplighter and downlighter to light a drawing board or large desk. If the work room includes VDUs, aim for glare-free lighting, and ensure book shelves, filing systems, etc are also adequately lit.

Above: *When working at a desk, do not position the lamp too high, or you will be working in your shadow.*

Above: *A lamp concealed over the desk will prevent dazzle and light the work surface clearly.*

Above and left: *A country-style utility room off a kitchen is used as a laundry, and a place for hobbies, as well as storage space for preserving equipment, vases etc. During the day the natural daylight is often adequate, but at night lighting is provided by spotlights on track which can be adjusted to give directional light.*

LIVING-ROOMS

As the living-room is probably the most important room in the house, you will want to induce specific moods with the lighting, and create an area which is relaxing and inviting. But it is also likely to be a multi-purpose room, so it is essential to plan a flexible lighting system. This will mean trying to have as many different circuits as possible to give maximum control, and it is wise to have the main general lighting circuit on a dimmer for even greater flexibility.

Choose your general background and accent lighting first, and then add the task lighting – reading lamps by a sofa; a desk lamp on a writing desk; lights on, or over a dining-table. You can use any one of the basic types of light source – downlighters, uplighters, wall-washers or the more traditional 'mix' of table and standard lamps with wall brackets, but unless the room is very large, don't use too many different types of light source.

Aim to create a warm inviting glow with the background lighting, which can be turned up or down depending on the type and time of day. If your room is furnished in a specific period style, then you may well opt for the 'mix' mentioned previously, with the actual fittings chosen to enhance the style of the decor. And some of these fittings could also provide task lighting (the table lamps, for example, doubling as reading lamps). Make these as flexible as possible by having plenty of socket outlets, so you can move lamps around and plug them in at will.

In a more modern setting, you could use uplighters, ceiling-recessed downlighters and some wall-washers. If these are discreet, and the room is of medium size, then there is no reason why these should not be combined with one or two period-style fittings.

Next consider accent or display lighting – use this to enhance plants or flowers; a favourite piece of furniture, or an ornament; an attractive architectural feature such as a fireplace, niche or alcove; a picture or wall-hanging; even the curtains, if they are in a particularly interesting fabric. The fittings you choose for this will also depend on the style of the room, but again the light source should be discreet – emphasizing the item rather than the fitting is the object of the exercise.

Once you have decided on the general and accent lighting, think about the various tasks which are performed in the room. If your dining-table is in the living-room, then you will want adequate lighting to enable diners to see to eat without being dazzled. You will need to light any serving-table or sideboard, and be able to plunge this area into darkness when the meal is over and you want to go into the sitting area to relax.

A pendant on a rise-and-fall fitting can double as general lighting as well as being pulled down specifically to light the dining-table, and in a large room, a similar lamp might be positioned over the coffee table at the other end of the room.

Other task lighting might include lamps for desk work, specific hobbies and pursuits. If your living-room contains a computer, note the comments on glare on page 14 – and remember not to position the television set so it reflects task lighting.

The living-room might also have to be used as a spare bedroom, with a sofa bed to accommodate overnight guests. In such rooms you will need even more socket outlets so you can plug in lamps as necessary to provide bedside lighting.

Above: *A centrally positioned pendant fitting in the living-room will cause a shadow.*

Above: *Angle a lamp behind a chair for efficient lighting.*

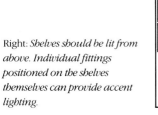

Right: *Shelves should be lit from above. Individual fittings positioned on the shelves themselves can provide accent lighting.*

Above: *The fireplace is a focal point in this cosy living-room – downlighters draw attention to the picture above the fireplace and accent the flower arrangement on the coffee table.*

Left: *Lighting in a child's room is provided by safe ceiling-recessed low-voltage downlighters which give good background lighting.*

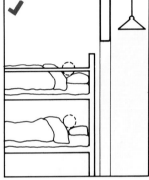

Above: *Children may feel more secure at night with some form of light source. A fitting on a dimmer switch in the hall is the perfect solution.*

BEDROOMS

The requirement for lighting bedrooms is not really very different from the living-room. Again it needs to be as flexible as possible, since you will want a certain amount of mood lighting and general soft background illumination. But you will also require functional lighting to see to dress and undress; at the dressing-table; and good lighting to see the page comfortably when sitting up to read in bed – but not so bright that it disturbs any sleeping partners.

You may also want to light any quiet 'sitting-out' area, and in the nursery, children's rooms, dual-purpose and bed-sitting-rooms, you will need task lighting for changing the baby, hobbies, homework or play. Make sure at least one light source is switched from the door, but again, different circuits would be advisable, since you want to be able to control the light to suit mood, function, and time of day.

In a small child's room you may need to make provision for a soft night-light – fitting a

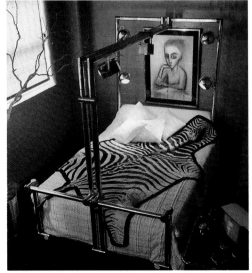

Above: *Spotlights are fixed to the metal frame of this very unusual bed in a hi-tech setting to illuminate the picture, provide bedside lighting and highlight the interesting textures.*

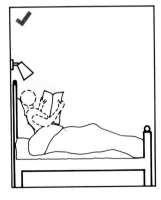

Above: *For reading in bed, a light positioned from behind will give a clear light.*

dimmer on the general background lighting may be sufficient, although there are special low-wattage lamps available.

Bedside lighting is frequently provided by lamps on bedside tables – one to each side of a double bed, which are individually switched. These should always be on a separate circuit from the rest of the bedroom lighting. But wall lights can be individually mounted above the bed (spots can work well here as they can be angled). Some sophisticated bedheads include integral lighting, and there are also fittings available which can be clipped to the bedhead.

Mirrors and the dressing table will need to be well lit. All too often these are positioned in a window for good daylight lighting, but at night (as with the kitchen sink) the lighting is woefully inadequate and you will be sitting in your own shadow. For the purpose of putting on make-up it is important to light the face, without glare or dazzle, and not to light the mirror. This can be done in various ways: with wall lights placed to each side of the mirror, with lamps on the dressing table, with a spotlight placed beside or behind the mirror which can be angled towards the face, and with the old 'favourite' of bulbs placed theatrical-style all round the mirror, although this last option is not the most efficient form of lighting, as light above the mirror tends to dazzle the eyes.

As with other rooms, the lamps on bedside tables, chests and dressing tables, and any wall lights or pendants can be in a style to suit the decor and period of the room, but the general or background lighting may well be provided by discreet downlighters, spotlights, wall-washers, and even uplighters. If you decide a pendant light will provide enough general background lighting in a small room, make sure you choose a fitting with an enclosed bulb, so you don't look up at it, and get glare from it when in bed.

Above: *Good dressing-table lighting is essential in the bedroom. Here, a small shadeless lamp lights the face from below in an art deco setting.*

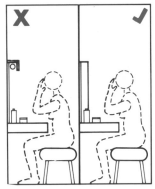

Left: *Mirrors should be lit from the side, not from above, otherwise the light will reflect off the mirror.*

SAFETY: CHILDREN'S ROOMS

One of the most important aspects to consider when lighting rooms for young children is safety. Plugs should be shuttered and leads on lamps be of the curly, retractable variety. Lamps should be positioned where they cannot be pulled over and lamp bases made of china (or other breakable material) should be avoided until children are older and more responsible.

BATHROOMS

Here the lighting needs to be similar to bedroom lighting – adequate task lighting for any mirror; good clear lighting for morning ablutions; and perhaps softer, more romantic lighting for a long soak in the evening. But lighting must also be safe since the combination of water, steam and electricity is potentially dangerous.

Portable lamps of any kind are extremely dangerous in bathrooms and are forbidden in some countries. Fittings should be covered with glass or plastic, leaving no exposed metal that can be affected by steam or condensation (so if you use the theatrical-style idea of bulbs round the mirror, these must be enclosed). Lights must be controlled from a switch outside the door (also any dimmer) or by a pull-cord switch. Lighting over bedroom basins should be similarly controlled. This means most spotlights, many uplighters and some downlighters cannot be used in the bathroom, but there are fully

recessed spill-ring downlighters which are particularly effective as they prevent glare from shiny surfaces such as ceramic tiles – and a gold reflector will give a warm touch to the most chilly of bathrooms.

Other suitable fittings include purpose-designed opaque discs, strips, globes and cubes – some of them with fluorescent tubes or bulbs or the spill-ring downlighters (mentioned above), some with tungsten-halogen downlighters, which will give a crisp, clear light. Showers need small, sealed special fittings. (Certain low-voltage downlighters with sealed glass covers can also be used above showers.) Mirrors can be lit with integral lighting or sealed strip lighting from above, or down the side.

There are special fittings which combine infra-red heating with a light, which can be mounted on the ceiling or wall and warm up the room, as well as providing light. These must be on a separate circuit and controlled by a pull-cord.

PLAY AND GAMES ROOMS

Today some bathrooms double as a gym or work-out room; some people plan their houses to make space for a separate playroom for their children; others are lucky enough to have room for a billiard, pool or table-tennis table. Most work-out rooms need some task lighting, but a soft, general background lighting is kinder when you are cycling nowhere!

The lighting design decisions will have to relate to the use of the room – billiard tables, for example, need special light fittings which illuminate the table evenly. There are several Victorian reproduction pendant fittings available, or you could use downlighters or spots on track mounted above the table. Other games tables may need good general background lighting, which might best be provided by recessed downlighters.

In children's playrooms many of the comments about children's bedrooms will apply. Any play or hobbies surface or a desk should be well lit, and be on a separate circuit from the general background lighting, which could be on a dimmer, especially if television is watched in this room.

CONSERVATORIES

Many people overlook the fact that conservatories need to be well lit, and forget to make provision for this in the planning, as the daylight lighting is usually good because of the glazing. In a very humid conservatory, the fittings should be condensation-proof, and in some cases garden lighting is a good alternative to interior domestic fittings.

At night, mood lighting will be all-important, and could be provided by uplighters hidden behind, or glowing through

Above: A conservatory which acts as an extension to the living-room and is used for summer dining has lantern-style pendants, uplighting for the plants and candlelight for dining.

plants. Candles also provide a romantic ambience for sitting or dining in a conservatory (the special garden and scented types are particularly suitable). If the conservatory is designed for special or several purposes, plan the lighting to relate – dining-tables lit from above; sitting areas with table lamps; plants and seedlings with special lighting arrangements if you want to 'bring them on' early. Many conservatory companies can provide advice and fittings, and you should not hesitate to discuss your lighting requirements with them.

TRICKS OF THE LIGHT

In most houses some of the rooms are less than perfect. They can be small, dark and cramped and lack natural daylight or be large, bleak and unwelcoming. Ceilings can appear too squat, or slope awkwardly. Some living-rooms, halls and corridors look too long and thin and seem to tunnel into the distance, while L-shaped rooms can create an impression of being 'hunched up'.

In some modern houses, the rooms may be square, bland and box-like, while in older properties (once decorated and furnished with large, impressive items) some areas appear far too tall when filled with today's lower-level furniture. And when larger properties are converted into apartments, the resulting rooms often resemble nothing more than tall thin tubes.

Other visual decorative problems can include awkward built-in items: ugly fireplaces; unsightly radiators and runs of pipes – all of which need to be camouflaged if they cannot be removed. On the plus side, there may be some beautiful features which you want to enhance: attractive original fireplaces; carefully crafted cornices and ceiling mouldings; or a beautifully shaped niche or window.

There are various ways of disguising unattractive features and drawing attention to the good ones, which include playing some decorating 'tricks' with the clever use of colour and pattern on the various surfaces. You can also use lighting to help you to achieve similar results, without resorting to costly structural alterations.

Just as sleight of hand needs constant practice, so playing decorating tricks involves proper advance planning. Look at your room as dispassionately as possible, evaluate the architectural style and decide on its good and bad features.

Right: *Four downlighters in a ceiling-mounted panel over the dining-table, combined with cleverly positioned accent lighting, emphasize the dining area in a living-room; the light is allowed to filter softly through a trellised screen, giving an impression of greater width and space to this L-shaped room.*

Above: *Lighting combined with mirrors creates an impression of greater width and endless space in what is, in reality, a fairly small, squarish hall.*

ALL DONE WITH MIRRORS

When a room lacks light, or depth, you can use mirrors to maximum effect to reflect both natural daylight and artificial light. Glass display shelves set in a recess, backed with mirrors and illuminated from above, below or the side, or with integral fittings as part of the shelving system, will maximize the available light, creating an interesting background glow and seemingly adding a whole new dimension to the room.

In a long, narrow hall or corridor, mirror glass covering one wall, illuminated from above (with ceiling-recessed downlighters, spots on track, or tubular lighting concealed behind a pelmet or baffle) will immediately look twice as large and light. The same trick will help in a small bathroom, but if you use mirror tiles here, make sure the wall surface is perfectly flat (or mount the tiles on chipboard and fix this to the wall) as slightly 'wobbly' reflective tiles will distort your image which can be particularly disconcerting in the bathroom.

If a whole wall of mirror is too overpowering, use panels of mirror. These can be left plain, or 'framed' in beading, a wallpaper border, or a stencilled design to suit your decorating scheme. Or use a strategically positioned, attractively shaped mirror, combined with a group of prints or pictures to make an eye-catching focal point on a blank wall.

In a really dark area (such as in an internal, windowless bathroom or on a dark landing), you can simulate a window with a panel of mirror or mirror tiles. You could even take this one stage further and fix a proper window frame to the wall and glaze with mirror instead of glass. Add 'dress' curtains with a pelmet or valance, with concealed lighting behind, to complete the illusion of light and space in a cramped area.

For a romantic touch in a dining-room or bedroom, there is nothing to compare with candlelight, magnified in a mirror. Position a mirror on the wall behind a chest, serving table or other suitable flat surface, or use a free-standing mirror. You might be lucky enough to find a triple-image mirror used on dressing tables in the 1920s and 30s to emphasize the glow further.

It takes two to judge just where to position a panel of mirror glass, or where to hang a mirror – one person to hold the mirror in position and the other to judge the effect. If you are also uncertain about the light source

Left: *A row of low-voltage eyeball downlighters, set into the window recess in a bedroom, illuminate the curtains at night. Reflector bulbs lessen the darkness of the fabric and emphasize the texture and a conventional table lamp throws a pool of light onto the bedside table. Both treatments draw the eye downwards, lessening the apparent height of the room.*

Below: *In an open space the lighting helps to 'zone' the areas, and to reduce the height. Ceiling-mounted spots and recessed downlighters are positioned to illuminate tables; wall hangings and pictures; sitting areas; and a storage and music centre, creating a more cosy ambience. Separate circuits provide maximum control, and some parts of the space can be completely dimmed out.*

in relation to a mirror, you will need two friends to help – one to hold the mirror and the other to move the light about (on a long lead) to judge the effect, and establish accurate positioning.

ALTERING SPACE

If you want to make your ceiling look taller, to 'flatten out' a slope or to create an impression of endless 'floating' space, you will need to use pale, cool colours and some slightly shiny textures, and to keep the use of pattern to a minimum on the main surfaces. You can then throw light up onto the ceiling, where it will be reflected and create an illusion of height. Use uplighters (which can be floor or wall-mounted) to achieve this result, or lighting concealed behind a cornice or baffle which runs all around the perimeter of the room. However, don't illuminate the ceiling in this way if the plaster is in poor condition as the light will show up every bump and crevice.

A background glow from lighting used in recesses and to light display shelves will also help to create this enlarging impression, and can be combined with mirrors as mentioned on the previous page.

If a central light fitting is essential, this might be the place to consider a crystal chandelier as this filters the light attractively and also 'bounces' light off the ceiling. Avoid any heavy pendant fittings – especially those with a closed top – as these will cast light downwards.

Plants or objects which appear to be 'floating' on a panel of glass, with the light softly diffused upwards will also create an illusion of space and height, so position them on a glass table, a panel of glass set into a built-in surface or on glass shelves. Light

Left: *Light is 'bounced' off the walls and sloping ceilings in this attic conversion forming interesting shapes and shadows which 'flatten out' the ceiling, making it appear higher and less claustrophobic, and at the same time creating an area of mystery and romance.*

them from below with individual uplighters or concealed lighting incorporated into the unit.

To make a room seem less lofty and to create an intimate mood, use warm colours and rough, soft or shaggy light-absorbing textures. Keep the light away from the ceiling, and if you must use a ceiling fitting, choose one which only directs the light downwards, suspended on a rise-and-fall fitting, which enables the height to be adjusted easily.

Draw attention to a low positioned feature in a high-ceilinged room – a picture, wallhanging, piece of sculpture, item of furniture, or the fireplace – or place objects or plants on a surface and light them dramatically from the side or above. Create 'pools' of light with table and standard lamps which give a warm glow to the area beneath them. In the kitchen, bathroom and bedroom,

light worktops, basins and dressing tables by wall-mounted fittings positioned about 60 cm (2 ft) above the surface, with the light directed downwards. Downlighters may also be concealed behind a pelmet or batten.

Coloured lights will provide an intimate, cosy ambience. Bulbs or shades in pinks, reds, burnt-orange, peach or golden yellow will give a warm glow to an otherwise austere interior, but remember to see these lit to judge the effect before purchasing. If you are using spots or downlighters choose the gold rather than the silver reflectors to give a warmer cast (*see* Theatrical Tricks page 24).

It is possible to use wall-washers, or recessed downlighters to bathe a wall area in comforting colour – if you want to be really sophisticated you can use different light filters on one system so you can change the colour of the wall at the flick of a switch to

suit your mood. Depending on your social life, you may want flashing strobe lighting for parties, although these are not particularly comfortable for daily living.

In a large area it is even more important to have as flexible a system as possible, with a choice of different light sources. Have each 'mood maker' on a separate circuit, and also fit dimmer switches where appropriate for even greater control. In a small home, try to take the eye through into the next room, or beyond, by using subdued illumination, or a light-accented item – this will help to increase the apparent size of the whole area.

If the living-room or hall is long and narrow, aim to increase the apparent width by focusing attention on the end wall or window, and 'washing' the other walls with an even light. Use a rich colour or boldly patterned wallcovering on the narrow end area, or a dramatic fabric for curtains. Alternatively, if this area is very narrow, you could decorate it with a picture, tapestry, wall hanging or other eye-catching item – or stand a piece of statuary on a plinth. If most of the area is taken up with a door, give this a *trompe l'oeil* treatment with paint or a mural.

Light any of these treatments for maximum effect. You could use ceiling-recessed downlighters; floor-mounted uplighters; spotlights on track above, or placed vertically down each side of a wall or window; or strategically placed wall-washers or wall-mounted uplighters with a tungsten-halogen linear bulb. Alternatively use pelmet lighting or a linear bulb concealed behind cornicing, a batten or a baffle. Make sure the colour rendition is good – (*see* page 13).

Right and below: *The flick of a switch can completely change the atmosphere in a room. In this living-room the lighting can be soft and clear for general purposes; draw attention to focal points such as the fireplace; and be dimmed right down for more intimate occasions.*

SHADOW PLAY

Lighting can also be used to throw shadows on walls, floors and ceilings, which will give the room an extra dimension. This is equally true with daylight as with artificial lighting. Light filtering through shutters, venetian blinds, sheer or open-weave fabrics or trellis-work screens, for example, is softened and made infinitely more interesting. Light shining through a stained-glass panel in the window or door creates wonderful coloured patterns, which change with the direction of the light. Consider these when planning a room and see if any of them can be incorporated with artificial light for added interest at night.

The outline of a large leafy plant or open-work trellis, thrown up onto the ceiling or across a wall to create a delicate filigree tracery will soften hard angles and make a box-like area seem more interesting and mysterious. Similarly, a light concealed behind louvres, a pierced screen, or sheer fabric can all enhance the atmosphere.

Accent lighting used to illuminate a specific object – a plant, a piece of statuary or a flower arrangement – dramatically lit, but angled to produce interesting contrasting shadows will provide a focal point. Don't forget the fireplace – this glowing centre of the room in winter can look dreary on other occasions and may well need alternative lighting, especially if you want to display plants, flowers or decorative objects on the hearth, in the fireplace opening or on the mantelpiece.

Left: *The shadows cast by foliage and star lanterns create an open airy atmosphere and add to the impression of space in a small area.*

Below: *An uplighter is used indoors to illuminate plants, creating a dramatic play of shadows against a blank wall.*

Above: *Light from a Moorish lantern throws interesting patterns up onto a richly coloured ceiling, helping to increase the impression of height.*

Above: *Decorating with light – in a simply furnished modern room, clever tricks of the light are used to throw a leafy pattern onto the wall, using low-voltage projectors fitted with shaped masks, special lenses and colour filters. Further accent lighting is used to enhance the picture.*

THEATRICAL TRICKS

There are many ways theatre, cinema and advertising hoarding lighting can be adapted to the domestic interior to create some stunning results. Most of these tend to suit a modern setting rather than a period one, and many of them demonstrate a tongue-in-cheek sense of humour.

The coloured filters previously mentioned, which will enable you to change the colour of a wall (and consequently the mood of the room) are adapted from theatrical 'gels' used for footlights and floodlights, and can be obtained from theatrical lighting specialists in literally hundreds of different colours.

The use of small circular light bulbs set into a wooden batten is often seen above or around dressing-table mirrors. These tend to light the mirror or wall rather than the face, so are not necessarily effective to make-up by, but will provide a glamorous accessory evocative of Hollywood. Don't use these in the bathroom though, unless the bulbs can be totally enclosed behind glass, or Perspex (acrylic) to make them waterproof. This idea can be adapted to outline other features, show a change in floorlevel or outline a bedhead. Use small 'golf ball'-type bulbs of low wattage to avoid glare and overheating, and if necessary fit with a diffuser.

On the same theme, there is a ready-made, flexible, clear plastic tubing available which contains small low-voltage light bulbs. This can be bought by length (it is 6 mm/¼ in square) from specialist lighting shops, and can be used to outline features. It is particularly good for defining treads or risers and preventing accidents on a dark stairway,

or for illuminating a change in floor levels. The strips can also be made into chandeliers, fixed to walls or around mirrors, doors, windows, bedheads or almost any other feature. They can even be hung across an opening like an illuminated bead curtain.

There are even more sophisticated techniques which can be used for dramatic effect. A projector, for example, similar to a framing projector (this includes a system of shutters and lenses which enables light to be shaped exactly to the dimensions of the item it is to accent), can be adapted to project light in a shape and throw this image onto walls, floors and ceilings. Some models incorporate a motor which moves the image round slowly.

Neon lighting is a form of strip lighting which was adapted from advertising hoardings and was frequently seen in cafés in the 50s. It comes in some attractive colours – and two or three different coloured narrow tubes are sometimes used to create a three-dimensional effect, and can be shaped interestingly to form unusual fittings.

Neon lighting works on very high voltage and requires transformers and a special kind of cable, but improvements are being developed all the time, and unusual items are readily available, such as green neon tube floor-standing lights, shaped like cacti or palm trees; pastel-coloured lights in the shape of cocktail glasses and bottles and various animal shapes and other ornaments. Neon tubing can also be shaped to fit around architectural features or mirrors. It gives a distinctly modern image and is best suited to modern, minimalist and hi-tech interiors or a teenager's bedroom, perhaps.

Left and above left: *Lighting tricks can be played with remote-controlled coloured filters or gels. This works best when the decor is in neutral colours, with interesting textures, which will reflect and absorb the light in different ways.*

The basic living-room, decorated in pale beige, cream and taupe, is lit for normal activities with a white light. A change of filter can create a cool green scheme; a warm pink-red one; an underwater blue-green; or, as here, a complementary combination of green and red, with accent on the fireplace.

FIXTURES AND FITTINGS

Light fittings have come a long way since the original invention of the incandescent light bulb by Edison in 1879, and many of today's fittings (like the low-voltage ones) have been designed, and manufactured, as a result of new developments in technology during the last 20 years.

Today fittings can provide many different types of light without the actual light source being noticed, so the light itself can be used as a decorating 'tool', and to create mood and atmosphere. However, in the past, lights and lamps were designed as decorative objects, and consequently became an integral part of the interior decoration. As has been said earlier, light fittings can still be chosen to echo the theme of a room, but it is essential not to see, or use, lighting merely as an accessory. The following pages will help you decide which fittings are most appropriate for specific functions.

Above: *This clamp-on lamp can be used in many different settings and would be ideal fixed above a desk in a study.*

TYPES OF FITTINGS

Light fixtures today are available in
an almost overwhelming range of
styles. Although this means there is
certain to be something to suit every
taste and budget, for those unfamiliar
with the market, the wide variety may
appear confusing. Working your way
through a lighting department or
specialist shop is much easier than
you think: although the styles and
prices may vary considerably, there
are actually only a few generic types of
fitting. Once you have decided what
type you are looking for – a pendant or
standard lamp, surface-mounted fitting
or wall-washer – it will make it easier
to explore the options available. This
chapter looks at the basic types of
lighting, while the chapter following,
Types of Lighting outlines how the
fixtures can be used to best effect.

Pendants and lanterns These are the types
of light which usually hang from the centre of
a ceiling (the original was a chandelier). They
can be a length of flex with a simple paper,
card or plastic shade; glass and metal lamps
and lanterns, which may be operated on a
rise-and-fall fitting which enables the light to
be raised or lowered at will; sophisticated
copies of gas or oil lamps in brass, steel and
opalescent glass; or even a conventional
chandelier.

Above: *This brass and glass pendant is a
copy of a Victorian hanging oil lamp and
would look good in a period setting.*

DESIGN DEVELOPMENTS

Historically, after-dark lighting was provided
by flaming torches; rush lights; early oil
lamps – originally made from hollowed-out
shells and then from terracotta; and later by
candles, which were placed on simple
candlesticks. These became more and more
sophisticated, with the development of
candle wall sconces, candelabra and
chandeliers.

The portable oil lamp – the Argand lamp
– was invented in France, using a wick
which was dipped in oil and which tended to
smoke. Later 19th-century developments
included lamps which burnt paraffin. This
transformed life in the evening, as work
could be carried on under the soft warm
glow of the lamp, and eventually even the
most modest households could afford several
such light sources.

Gas lighting was developed about 1850
as street lighting, but was then adapted to
the domestic interior, with gas piped into the
house for use in wall and central lights and
also table lamps. All these systems needed
constant attention – and there was a
constant fire hazard.

In the 1890s the potential of electric light
in the domestic setting began to be
appreciated by leading architects who
experimented with designs which
incorporated light as an integral part of the
building structure. As new materials like
plastic, steel, aluminium, chrome and
toughened glass emerged in the 1920s and
30s, light fittings began to be 'designed' as
features in their own right.

In the last 20 years things have changed
dramatically, with background and
atmospheric lighting cast on various
surfaces from almost invisible sources. But
there are still plenty of decorative fittings
available, from reproductions of Victorian
oil and gas lamps; art deco and Tiffany-style
wall lights and table lamps; 30s standard
lamps to modern uplighters and metal
hi-tech fittings. These can be used to provide
task and some background lighting.

Left: *Neat metal pendants can be ceiling-
mounted, preferably on a rise-and-fall
fitting so they can be pulled down over a
surface to provide task lighting.*

Surface-mounted fittings These lights are fitted to the wall or ceiling, and can be in almost any style from black cast-iron 'Tudor' to modern fittings in plastic, metal or wood. Some are mounted on armatures, and require separate shades which are usually chosen to suit the style of the bracket, or fitted flush to the wall, and which include totally enclosed globes. They can be fitted above eye level as uplighters or mounted the opposite way, as downlighters. Others can be ceiling-mounted, although these are less flexible than pendants, and can be flush to the ceiling. Alternatively, the actual fitting (usually metal) may hold one or more lamps, which often have matching wall lights. Spotlights (on or off track) can also be classed as ceiling-mounted fittings.

Table lamps These are infinitely versatile forms of lighting, and come in all shapes, sizes, colours and styles. Some have separate shades, and others have the shade as an integral part of the lamp. Bases and shades are often sold separately, so you can choose your own shade to suit the base and the decor. Always test the shade on the base for effect and 'balance' before buying. As a general rule, the shade should be at least as tall as the base – and wide enough to throw a pool of light onto the surface below – but not so wide that it looks over-balanced. Always check the maximum wattage the light will accept, and ensure the bulb is not too big (or hot) for the chosen shade. Air should be able to circulate round the bulb to prevent scorching the shade. Remember to check the colour of the shade, lit and unlit to make sure it will look as well with your scheme during the day as at night.

Above: *Mains voltage track-mounted spotlight, fitted with a tungsten-halogen high intensity lamp.*

Above: *A surface-mounted picture light will provide traditional accent lighting and can be fixed to any wall.*

Right: *Candle-type table lamps in metal and wood for every room in the house.*

Standard lamps These are tall, freestanding fittings which use an ordinary incandescent bulb and can be made from metal, wood, or plastic, and can be moved around at will. Styles vary and there are many different shades to suit. Again these need to look well-balanced with the lamp, and to be wide enough to shed the right degree of light. Some come in sets to match table, ceiling and wall fittings. A modern development is the uplighter on its own slim stand.

Right: *A sophisticated uplighter on a metallic stand can be used in a variety of different rooms and situations, and is easily portable.*

Below: *A selection of different-sized incandescent bulbs used in table, pendant and wall fittings, with bayonet or screw-in fixing. The candle-type are recommended for use in wall or table lamps and chandeliers where they are partially on view. Coloured bulbs give a warm glow, creating an impression of candlelight.*

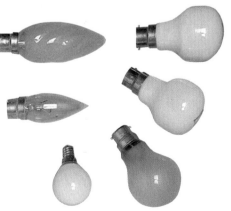

Left: *Lighting for reading, embroidery and other close work should be kind on the eyes and not throw any shadows. One of the best ways is to have a lamp behind a favourite chair or sofa, as here, which can be adjusted to the correct height. The soft opalescent shade allows the light to glow through without glare.*

Uplighters These direct a beam of light up onto the ceiling, lighting the room indirectly, and again, they come in various styles which can be selected to suit the room theme. Some are designed to be wall-mounted, and should be positioned high enough up to prevent glare, and the bulb should be shaded. Others are on slim stands. There are smaller versions available which can be floor-standing and used to illuminate plants, paintings and statuary. These often use tungsten-halogen bulbs and reflectors which give a clear bright white light, and some are low-voltage.

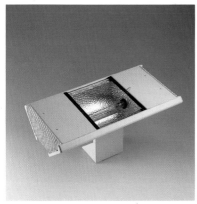

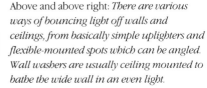

Above and above right: *There are various ways of bouncing light off walls and ceilings, from basically simple uplighters and flexible-mounted spots which can be angled. Wall washers are usually ceiling mounted to bathe the wide wall in an even light.*

Left: *Tungsten-halogen bulbs used in special fittings – the linear type are designed for use in wall-mounted uplighters and some standard lamps.*

Downlighters These are recessed in the ceiling or ceiling-mounted as part of the structure, and shine downwards to give either general or specific light. Screw-in bulbs or eyeball fittings with mini-reflector bulbs which can be swivelled to shed light wherever it is needed may be used. Some are semi-recessed and have a type of shade in the form of a band of material (usually glass or metal) protruding from the ceiling. Many fittings are now low-voltage.

Above and above left: *Recessed downlighters, both low-voltage, and high output with integral reflectors. Reflectors are also available in gold, which casts a warmer light, and may be used to enhance a room with a 'cold' atmosphere.*

Left: *Examples of low-voltage 'lamps' – the bulbs used in low-voltage fittings, some of which come with their own reflectors. Make sure the correct size is used for the fitting and don't handle them with bare hands.*

Wall-washers These are ceiling-mounted and are more obvious than downlighters. Part of the aperture is masked by a reflective surface which directs the beam of light towards the wall, effectively 'washing it' with light. They are designed to cast light evenly across and down the wall, and emphasize the vertical surfaces rather than the horizontal ones of floor, table or ceiling. They can be used to give a clear, even light to illuminate the wall treatment – including paintings and mirrors – and some are low-voltage.

Spotlights Spots project light in a definite direction, and are designed to be used with a variety of bulbs to provide different types of beam, from very narrow, to illuminate specific items, to very wide floods, for large items. They come singly; on fixed or flexible track; as clusters; in different colours and finishes; and can be fitted to almost any surface. Some can be swivelled and angled, while others are fixed fittings.

PRACTICAL CONSIDERATIONS

Once you have an idea of what fittings you want, and where they should be positioned, you will need to check just how feasible installation will be. Most homes have plastered walls and ceilings, which makes the changing of centre light fittings, and the inserting of wiring and cables in the walls fairly easy, but really old lath-and-plaster walls, or modern plasterboard ones may create problems. Discuss this with your electrician, and make sure you are both agreed exactly where everything should go.

Some modern buildings have concrete ceilings, and it is impossible to cut holes in these, so if you want downlighters, these cannot be recessed. Surface-mounted ones are a feasible alternative, and it is sometimes possible to put a panel on the ceiling to hide the built-in transformer which is part of low-voltage fittings. But a point to remember is that the ceiling of an apartment is the floor of somebody else's home. There is no point in putting lighting into the ceiling if you cannot have guaranteed access, should the lighting need attention.

Any fittings which have to be installed as part of the structure should be in position before decorating is done, so any channelling-out of walls, or holes in ceilings must be cut, filled and made good first. It helps to have this main lighting in position before you finally select your colours, floor, wall and window treatments, so you can look at the samples under the exact lighting conditions.

Below: *The mini-fitting below creates the magical effect of a star-studded ceiling for general lighting, giving a quality of lighting similar to uplighting, but with a very simple semi recessed ceiling fitting which takes a tungsten-halogen bi-pin lamp. The fitting is held in the ceiling with a pin and uses the ceiling itself as a reflector.*

Above: *Mains voltage adjustable spotlight with built-in shields to dispel heat away from the lamp fitting.*

Above: *Single circuit spotlight – different models provide varieties of beam width. A 'pencil' beam is effective for accent lighting.*

TYPES OF LIGHTING

In order to plan your lighting properly and efficiently, reach design decisions or play any visual 'tricks', you need to understand the various different types of lighting. Basically there are three main types of lighting – general or background lighting, task lighting, and accent or display lighting. There are many ways in which these can be provided, but it is important to remember that most rooms need a combination of types, and some rooms may need all three. The living-room, for example, will need overall background lighting for general use, and well-positioned task lighting for activities such as reading, sewing and so on. The following pages look at the fixtures that are best suited for each type of light.

Above: *Sometimes accent or task lighting can be dimmed to provide a background glow. Here spotlights on track can be angled to provide good light for sewing or reading. They also provide general background lighting.*

Above: *General lighting in a dining area is provided by a pendant and spotlights on track. The spots provide flexible lighting, too, and can be angled to accent details.*

BASIC TYPES OF LIGHTING

General or background lighting
This provides the overall brightness in a room, for general purposes.

Task lighting
General lighting is not sufficient to allow for specific tasks like reading, desk work, sewing, and cooking, so an additional light source must be provided.

Accent or display lighting
This is used to accentuate points of interest such as flowers, pictures or plants.

GENERAL OR BACKGROUND LIGHTING

When people think of lighting, this is probably the type that most immediately springs to mind as it provides the overall illumination in any area. It is important that the background lighting scheme is given as much thought and planning as more specialized types, as it will influence the atmosphere of the room. General or background lighting can be provided in several different ways.

TRADITIONAL FITTINGS

Pendants These are the utilitarian fittings found hanging from, and usually in the centre of, the ceiling in most domestic interiors. They tend to give an inadequate light, leaving the edges of the room in shadow.

A pendant can be modified by the choice of shade – a wide conical shade, upturned to reflect light back onto the ceiling for example; or a hemisphere of glass, plastic and even the popular Oriental translucent paper 'lanterns' will produce a softer light.

A more up-market version of the pendant is the chandelier. These originally held candles, providing a flickering light which was magnified a hundredfold by the glittering glass of the fitting. Now converted to electricity, the resulting light is somewhat harsher. Lower wattage bulbs of the candle type are recommended to reduce glare. When installing a chandelier, remember they are very heavy and chains and hooks should be very strong and firmly secured to a ceiling joist. This type of light can look very attractive in a traditional setting in a dining-room.

There are other lights which can be used to illuminate a dining-table – these come in lots of different designs, and are shaped to throw an attractive glow onto the table. This type of light is best installed on a rise-and-fall fitting which allows you to pull it down or push it up as necessary. If you have a long dining-table, you may need two such lights positioned to illuminate both ends.

One of the best ways of lighting a dining-table is by downlighters, positioned in, or surface-mounted on the ceiling, so that the beams cross, to provide an even illumination for the entire surface. Remember that lights over tables should be positioned so they light the main area of the table and don't shine into the eyes of the diners.

There are other 'fancy' types of centre light, such as those combined with ceiling fans for ventilation. These can be effective in the right setting, such as a conservatory filled with rattan furniture.

A point worth remembering is that if you have a pendant fitting in a bedroom, choose a shade which encloses the bulb. This way you won't get a view of the bulb or any glare when lying in bed.

Left: *This metal, chandelier-style pendant can be used with electric candles to provide general lighting, or real candles for romantic evenings. It looks particularly effective in a conservatory, hall or over a dining-table.*

Wall lights These are a traditional way of providing general or background lighting, although they rarely do more than provide a background glow. They can be simple wall brackets and sconces, which require small shades and are usually an integral part of the decorating scheme. Use the recommended wattage for the shade to avoid scorching or possible fire hazard.

There are many 'improved' wall fittings on the market which use a linear tungsten-halogen bulb. The light is thrown up to the ceiling and reflected down again, giving excellent illumination. When wall lights are installed ensure they are positioned about two-thirds up the wall – high enough up (not less than 2 m/6 ft) to prevent glare and view of the bulb. Consequently, in a low-ceilinged room, wall lights may not be practical.

Table and standard lamps Although these are often used to provide task lighting, more often than not they are also used to give a background glow of general lighting to a room as they throw attractive pools of light onto various surfaces. Table and standard lamps come in all shapes, styles and sizes, and are usually chosen as an accessory to suit the style of the room. It is important to balance the size and shape of the shade with the height and style of the base or standard. Always try to take a lamp with you when shopping for a shade, or make an 'on approval' arrangement with the supplier.

INTEGRAL FITTINGS
Downlighters These are usually recessed in the ceiling, but can be surface-mounted if cutting holes in the ceiling is not feasible. They can be mains or low-voltage, and usually combine reflectors in gold or silver – the choice will depend on the colour scheme of the room. Make sure these are installed in the correct position for the purpose for which they are intended.

Above: *Pastel-coloured bulbs are used in two table lamps, and a 100 watt bulb is used in the pendant fitting which provides general background lighting in this living-room.*

Right: *Downlighters positioned above the unit and lavatory light the mirror and basin clearly.*

Far right: *Wall-mounted downlighting on a twisting staircase lights the edge of the treads.*

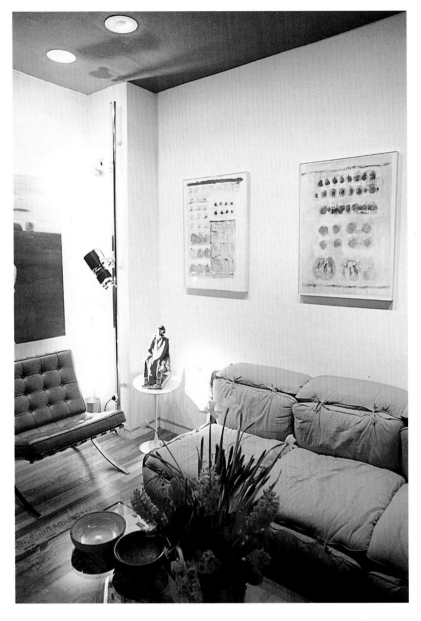

Above: *Downlighters and uplighters provide general background lighting in this modern living-room.*

NEWER TYPES OF FITTINGS

Uplighters These can be floor or wall-mounted or a version of the standard lamp, and can be low or mains voltage. The floor or standard type are easily portable, and thus provide very flexible lighting. This type of lighting can often double as accent or display lighting and is particularly effective when combined with plants.

Wall-washers These bathe the walls in a glow of light, providing a very airy impression. They tend to 'push the walls out', so creating an impression of greater space, and can also provide colour interest.

Above: *Uplighters come in different shapes and sizes. They usually have a distinctive style and become an integral part of the room scheme. They provide effective background or accent lighting.*

DIMMING SYSTEMS

Many general or background lighting fittings are more effective and efficient if combined with a dimming system. This would need checking with the electrician, and in some cases several separate circuits may be advisable.

At least one circuit of general background lighting should be able to be switched on upon entering the room, and in some cases needs to be dual-switched (for example in hall, stair or landing areas).

TASK LIGHTING

This is usually provided by lamps which can be controlled to light a required surface. Make sure the wattage output is suitably high to supply a clear light, without glare or dazzle. When lighting mirrors for making-up or shaving, ensure the light shines on the face and does not 'bounce' off the mirror.

Among the many forms of task lighting are the following:

Shaded fluorescent Most fluorescent tubes are rather harsh, but in a hobby area, sited over a workbench, for example, they give a good, clear light, although they must be shaded. If used to light a kitchen work surface, they are usually fitted under the bottom of a wall-mounted cupboard above the worktop, or behind a batten.

Fluorescent tubes can also be concealed behind a coving or batten going around the perimeter of a room, to throw light up onto the ceiling. They can be used as display (accent) lighting, when they are incorporated into cabinets, shelves or units or as 'pelmet' lighting – now considered rather old-fashioned. Fluorescent tubes may be used to illuminate pictures, but they are not as effective as other forms of accent lighting.

Above: *Ceiling-recessed eyeball spots light a country-style kitchen unobtrusively. Additional task lighting is provided by fluorescent tubes concealed underneath wall-mounted cabinets.*

Above: *Bedside lighting needs to be adjusted to various tasks – the most usual is to ensure the light falls comfortably onto the page when sitting up in bed reading without dazzling a sleeping partner. Here the size of lamp and shade have been carefully calculated so the pool of light is angled correctly.*

Left: *An unusual fitting suspended above the bed gives a really clear light for reading or breakfasting in bed.*

Above: *A workshop in a garage has natural daylight provided by the partially glazed roof. At night task lighting is provided by spotlights mounted on track.*

Track lighting, combined with spotlights

This is basically an elongated electric socket, which enables several lights to be attached along its length making it possible for an existing electrical source to supply a number of separate fittings without costly installation. The spots can then be angled towards various surfaces to provide task lighting in addition to an element of general background lighting.

Track lighting can be ceiling- or wall-mounted – even floor-mounted in some instances, and can be mains or low-voltage. Live track enables spotlights to be plugged in, and slid into position at any point along the length of the track fitting; fixed-bar track has a predetermined number of spots along the length which are not adjustable.

LOW-VOLTAGE LIGHTING

This is a popular and readily available form of lighting. It involves the use of a transformer to bring the mains voltage (240 volts in the UK and 100 volts in the US) down to 6, 12 or 24 volts – over 90 per cent of low-voltage fittings currently in use run at 12 volts (like a car battery). The transformer has to be connected to the circuit, and positioned in a practical place, where it can be reached easily if any work has to be done on it. Today, many low-voltage fittings have a transformer built in as part of the design, without making them too bulky, but check and allow for this when arranging for installation.

Left and above left: *A freestanding, low-voltage uplighter is used to accent a painting.*

ACCENT AND DISPLAY LIGHTING

This can be provided by many of the lighting systems listed previously – alcove and display lighting is even more effective if combined with glass shelves, and the light can travel through the glass.

Track lighting and well-planned downlighters can be positioned to shine directly down onto a coffee table, or an area with an arrangement of ornaments or flowers on it. They can be used to illuminate pictures and wall-hangings far more effectively than the 'traditional' picture light. Floor- and wall-mounted uplighters can illuminate a flower arrangement, plants (these look even more dramatic if grouped on a glass-topped table with the light shining up through it), or a piece of statuary. In a sophisticated setting a framing projector can be used.

Low-voltage lighting also comes into its own here. Because of the nature of the fittings and the light beam, a much more dramatic effect can be created – the beam is more tightly controlled, with the source supplied by much more discreet fittings.

PLANNING TIP

When electrical work is being done, always plan for the optimum requirements. This is equally true whether you are installing power points in a kitchen (always put in at least twice as many as you first thought of, and always double sockets), or planning the lighting for any main room. Plan ahead and provide as many light sources as the room will eventually require – on several circuits to make it easier to control.

Above: *Spotlights can be used effectively as display and accent lighting. A spot mounted on metal tubing is adjustable, and can be moved up or down to vary the angle of light.*

Above: *A cluster of three spots, surface-mounted on a hall ceiling, light the table, picture and staircase.*

OUTDOOR AND SECURITY LIGHTING

Exterior lighting used to be confined to the front and back door, with possibly a modest glow on the patio. Today, illuminating the garden can be as comprehensive as the interior lighting – and chosen to perform similar functions of background and accent lighting – as well as providing a safe environment after dark.

Outdoor lighting can be used to highlight trees, statues, groups of plants in pots, and other features; to give a basic background glow for night-time walks; to floodlight an attractive façade or weathered wall; to provide an interesting vista effect from inside the house; and to light barbecues and outdoor dining-tables on patios or balconies for night-time dining. Strings of coloured lights can also be effective for parties on summer evenings or used to decorate a tree or part of the garden at Christmas. A special weather-proof socket can be a permanent feature, and the lights taken in and stored when not needed.

DRAMA WITHOUT DAZZLE

Artificial night lighting shows off shapes and aspects of trees, shrubs, walls, trellises, and other features in a way not normally seen by day – which is all part of the magic. It will give the garden a completely different atmosphere in the evening from during the daytime.

Remember that outdoors a little lighting goes a long way – you won't want the entire garden flooded with light. This is just as well, since the fittings and wirings are more costly than their indoor equivalents. But a small number of lights will create an atmosphere of mystery and intrigue as will lighting one or two features dramatically. And as exterior light appears brighter than it would indoors, low-wattage bulbs (ie a PAR 38 bulb) are more effective.

In order to test out the effect of garden lighting, and to decide the position of the fittings, take a walk around the grounds at night with a torch (flashlight) – and a friend. Use several torches of different sizes, with different light beams if you are aiming to create different moods. While one of you lights various areas and features to judge the effect, the other can look at them from inside the house, the end of the garden, the patio, the back door, and even from the road and neighbouring gardens to make sure you are not going to dazzle anybody.

Left: An imposing entrance, steps and door are defined with a porch light, plus concealed spotlights with flood bulbs.

Left: *Floods and spots feature trees, shrubs and terrace at the back of a house.*

Above: *Flexible garden lighting bathes an al fresco table with light for dining, accents climbing shrubs and enhances low-growing plants. Besides creating evening enchantment and enabling the garden to be enjoyed to the full on warm summer evenings, it also provides safety and security.*

Aim for flexibility and possible seasonal changes. You may, for example, have a shrub which is beautifully shaped from spring through autumn, but which is pruned back in the winter. However some evergreens and other trees (silver birch, willow or cornus for example) look just as attractive in winter when they are leafless, and their almost architectural form can be fully appreciated when illuminated, or 'back lit' dramatically so the silhouette stands out against the sky or background.

A mercury vapour source light produces a distinctly bluish light for a magical 'frosty' effect. White light also looks very effective against a dark background, but coloured bulbs can help to add extra interest to some features. Green bulbs will emphasize a group of green plants and shrubs; blue can look good in some garden pools; and red will add a welcoming glow to a patio, a brick wall or a grouping of terracotta pots, or may be used to illuminate a red or bronze-leafed shrub to

contrast with a dark background. Don't forget that if you bathe the barbecue area in a red light you will probably overcook the meat, since it will stay looking red and succulent when it is really well-cooked.

You can prepare a lighting plan for the garden in a similar way to a room plan, by measuring up and drawing out the garden to scale and plotting the positions for the various fittings to relate to the features which you want to illuminate (*see* Planning and Measuring Up pages 6–9). But remember trees and plants will grow, so the view will change from year to year, and the lighting plan must accommodate this.

PRACTICAL ASPECTS

As outdoor light sources are mostly positioned at ground or eye level, they must not be allowed to dazzle. Light sources can be hidden behind a baffle and diffused, or have some other form of glare control. Many modern fittings have this built in, with anti-

glare cowls or louvres as standard accessories, so check this before ordering.

For safety's sake all exterior fittings should be capable of withstanding the weather for years. Metalwork should be protected against corrosion; the bulb-holder and connectors must be completely sealed against dust and damp; and the bulbs should be made from weatherproof toughened glass, like the PAR 30 bulb, for example.

Any outdoor lighting circuit should be separate from the interior one, and you may need to install more than one in a large garden. Outdoor circuits should be run from special exterior-quality cable, and the circuit should be isolated at least 45 cm (18 inches) underground. For safety's sake, this cable must be protected in conduit so it cannot be weakened or disturbed by animals. Employ a properly qualified electrician to do the work and install the cables and fittings – this is not a do-it-yourself job.

SECURITY FACTOR

Good exterior lighting will also contribute to safety and security. If steps, paths and patios are adequately illuminated, this will prevent falls and accidents. The very fact you have exterior lighting can also act as a deterrent to would-be intruders, as well as providing a welcome for friends and family.

Part, if not all, of the entire circuit could also be controlled on a time switch to come on automatically at dusk. This is particularly useful when you are away on holiday. Some time controls are so sophisticated they can be programmed to switch on and off at different times each evening, or to come on earlier or later as the seasons change.

There are also special security lights available, some of which work on a heat sensor, which come on automatically when the house is approached. Some can be programmed to stay alight for a certain length of time while others switch off almost at once. Many models look rather like spotlights,

or have an 'industrial' image, but there are now some attractive fittings designed for the porch and front door, which look like old-fashioned lanterns or other traditional fittings or glowing globes, and can be selected to suit the architectural style of the house.

You may decide to install one of these at both the front and back door, or to put a double fitting on the garage or at the side of the house. Automatic security lights need to be carefully sited (again, do a test before fixing) so you don't create dazzle in the bedrooms, or in neighbouring houses. Some of these lights are so sensitive they can come on in the middle of the night when a car passes along the road.

Note: It is wise to have the security lighting separately switched from the decorative garden lighting, and to site it carefully, so it won't keep coming on and off when friends and family are enjoying the garden in the evening – or when the neighbours are sitting out in theirs.

ZONING THE AREAS

When it actually comes to deciding on the type of light fittings and levels of light, you will find that lighting a garden is as interesting, and the choice almost as varied, as lighting a large room – and you will need the equivalents of task, background and accent lighting.

GARDEN FEATURES

If you are lighting garden features – like plants, shrubs, trees or statuary – apply the same principles as accent lighting inside. Choose the subjects carefully and light with an eye for form and contrast, and shadow-play. White flowers look particularly magical when lit at night, so a rambling white rose, wall-climbing jasmine, clump of white lilies or silver-leafed shrub are well worth accenting.

Try an outdoor spotlight with spike base to bury in the ground, which can be used with either a spot bulb (for smaller plants) or a flood bulb (for a larger area or plants), and

Right: *An outdoor spotlight is a flexible light source if it has a spike base. You can move it to enhance different features as the seasons change, or angle it as plants grow taller and larger. The PAR 38 outdoor spotlight can be used with either a spot or flood bulb.*

Above: *Simple lighting can be as effective in the garden as floods and spots. Storm lanterns, designed for use with candles, have clear glass covers, so the wind won't extinguish the flame. They also provide a warm intimate glow for summer dining – in a conservatory as well as on the terrace.*

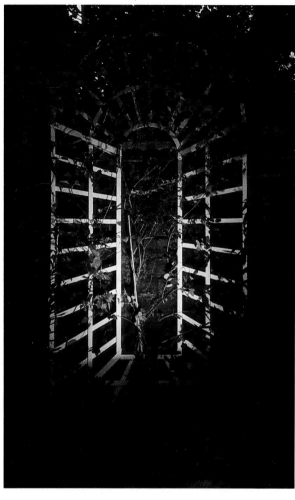

Above: *A magical corner in a small city garden is created by the clever use of a white-painted trellis shaped to form an arch. It is lit at night by spotlights with flood bulbs.*

which can be moved around. Other fittings can be buried in a pot amongst a group of planters. Low-voltage fittings using a 12 volt PAR 36 bulb are successful for subtle garden lighting and for smaller items. But, as with interior low-voltage fittings, transformers must be used. A group transformer can power several such fittings, but must be placed in a sheltered position and there will be special cable requirements. Some exterior low-voltage fittings are available with built-in transformers.

PATHS, TERRACES, PATIOS AND PORCHES
Areas close to the house or which perform a certain function require special lighting. The patio, terrace, or any other area immediately outside a large window has to link the bright light indoors with the dark night outside, but the inside light will help to light the patio indirectly, so remember this in your planning. Try burying lights in pots on the terrace or in bordering flowerbeds or conceal a spotlight in

foliage climbing up a wall or a trellis. Light the table with candles or hurricane lamps (shielded from the wind) or a spot mounted on the wall or in a tree above, but make sure it will not shine into the eyes of the diners. Candles in long spiked holders can also be dotted in amongst plant pots and in flowerbeds for special occasions, and strings of coloured lights can be festooned around the patio area. These may be hired if you don't have a set.

If your house has interesting architectural features, you can use wall fittings which act as both downlighters and uplighters, shining upwards to light the feature and downwards to illuminate the terrace or path. These may also be used in tall trees, or on garden walls if there is a climbing plant above and a feature on the wall, (or in the beds or terrace below) worth illuminating.

Paths and steps may need task lighting. A tall, standard lamp – perhaps a converted or reproduction old-style street lamp – is a popular light source, as is a lantern fixed on the side of the house. There is also a wide range of specialized step lights – bollards which glow like pieces of crystal or overhead hanging lights which will create the right atmosphere while providing a safe environment. Sometimes, simply concealing spotlights in bordering flowerbeds will supply adequate light to outline the steps clearly.

Make sure the number of your house is clearly illuminated, and use task lighting for gates, front doors and porches. Again, choose these to suit the architectural style of the house. You may find the security lighting previously discussed is sufficient for the front door, but you may need an additional light source for the name plate.

The conservatory often leads out into the garden, and if it is cleverly lit it can look magical from outside, and still help to throw a little general background lighting onto a lawn or terrace. This is why sun-room and conservatory lighting should be planned to be as flexible as possible – so it can be dimmed for intimate wining and dining; to accent 'architectural' plants; perhaps to help with growing special plants and seedlings; and to provide a link between garden and house.

Above and left: *Lighting up the garden path – and the driveway, steps and other irregular surfaces – will prevent accidents, and enable you to enjoy the great outdoors at night. The bollard-shaped light can be used to illuminate drives, paths and steps. The globe lights are low-voltage, designed for the more traditional garden.*

ADDITIONAL TASK LIGHTING

Don't forget the greenhouse, shed and garage! When you are planning your garden lighting, these areas are often forgotten, but it helps to have adequate task lighting in outside buildings, so you can do a little work on the car or prick out a few seedlings after dark, and in the garage you may well need a power supply for tools. Cables to such buildings need to be properly insulated and buried as with any other outdoor lighting.

LIGHTING WATER

Lighting water features and swimming pools creates a wonderful effect at night, especially if the pool is a Mediterranean blue. The lights should be set below the level of the water and around the perimeter of the pool to define its shape. This means purpose-made waterproof fittings should be installed at the same time as the pool, to keep wiring clear of the water. It is essential that this is discussed with the installers at the planning stage.

If the pool has buildings, such as a pool house, or a colonnade or pergola close by, these might be illuminated to throw reflections onto the water and give background glow. This lighting should be separately switched so the pool can be kept dark and mysterious when the surrounding area is illuminated.

Ornamental garden pools and ponds are also best lit by low-voltage fittings submerged

in the water, but again, these must be waterproof and fitted when the pool is being installed. Rainproof spotlights can also be used, with their beam angled to shine just above water level. In some cases, spots can be hidden in the foliage and plants surrounding the pool, so these present attractive silhouettes against the water.

Fountains and cascades can be lit for dramatic effect so the water sparkles like a liquid chandelier. This can be done by submerged waterproof narrow-beam sources set close to the base of each jet, or shining along it. Some fountains (especially those for indoor use in conservatories) come complete with built-in lighting fittings.

Above: *A lantern-shaped shaded light can be positioned at the side of the gate or doorway or used to accent features in a walled garden.*

Left: *Garden pools look magical at night if they are well lit. These pond lights are low-voltage and can be submerged, or used as surface lighting for pools and waterfalls. They can be fitted with red, blue, green or amber lenses to change the mood.*

BULB AND LAMP CHART

The bulbs described in the following chart are all suitable for domestic use, and give a good example of the wide range available. Please note that manufacturers may offer slight variations on the generic types.

Note: Mains voltage is 240 in the UK, and 100 in the US. Bulb caps refer to the bayonet fitting (BC) and standard Edison screw. The bulb life is given in hours.

TUNGSTEN	DESCRIPTION	WATTAGE	VOLTAGE	CAP	BULB LIFE	BEAM ANGLE
	standard incandescent or GLS (general lighting service)	40	main	E27/BC	1000	
		60	main	E27/BC	1000	
		100	main	E27/BC	1000	
		150	main	E27/BC	1000	
		200	main	E27/BC	1000	
	globe	25	main	E27	2000	
		40	main	E27	2000	
		60	main	E27	2000	
		100	main	E27	2000	
		150	main	E27	2000	
	golf-ball or 'spherical'	40	main	E14/BC	1000	
	crown-silvered bulb	40	main	E14	1000	
		60	main	E27	1000	
		100	main	E27	1000	
	ISL (internally silvered reflector bulb)	40	main	E14/E27	1000	35°
		60	main	E27	1000	80°
		60	main	E27	1000	35°
		75	main	E27	1000	35°
		75	main	E27	1000	100°
		100	main	E27	1000	35°
		150	main	E27	1000	35°
	PAR 36 (parabolic aluminized reflector bulb)	25	12	Screw	2000	8° × 10°
		50	12	Screw	2000	9° × 11°
		30	6	Screw	1000	3.5°
	PAR 38 spot	75	main	E27	2000	15°
	flood	75	main	E27	2000	40°
	spot	100	main	E27	2000	15°
	flood	100	main	E27	2000	40°
	spot	150	main	E27	2000	15°
	flood	150	main	E27	2000	40°
	spot	60	main	E27	2000	12°
	flood	60	main	E27	2000	30°
	spot	80	main	E27	2000	12°
	flood	80	main	E27	2000	30°
	spot	120	main	E27	2000	12°
	flood	120	main	E27	2000	30°
	PAR 56 narrow-beam	300	main	G × 16d	2000	10° × 16°
	medium-beam	300	main	G × 16d	2000	13° × 26°
	wide-beam	300	main	G × 16d	2000	18° × 34°
	standard strip-light	30	main	S15s	1000	
		60	main	S15s	1000	
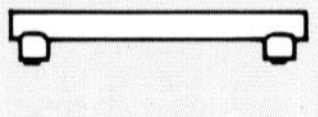	strip-light or 'linear' bulb	35	main	S14s	1000	
		60	main	S14s	1000	
		120	main	S14s	1000	

FLUORESCENT	DESCRIPTION	WATTAGE	VOLTAGE	CAP	BULB LIFE	LENGTH	DIAMETER
	standard (triphosphor or halophosphate)	15	main	G13	7000	450mm/18in	26mm/1in
		30	main	G13	7000	900mm/3ft	26mm/1in
		20	main	G13	7000	600mm/2ft	26mm/1in
		18	main	G13	7000	600mm/2ft	26mm/1in
		40	main	G13	7000	1200mm/4ft	26mm/1in
		36	main	G13	7000	1200mm/4ft	26mm/1in
		65	main	G13	7000	1500mm/5ft	26mm/1in
		58	main	G13	7000	1500mm/5ft	26mm/1in
		75/85	main	G13	7000	1800mm/6ft	26mm/1in
		70	main	G13	7000	1800mm/6ft	26mm/1in
		125	main	G13	7000	2400mm/8ft	26mm/1in
		100	main	G13	7000	2400mm/8ft	26mm/1in
	miniature	4	main	G5/15	5000	150mm/6in	16mm/½in
		6	main	G5/15	5000	225mm/9in	16mm/½in
		8	main	G5/15	7500	300mm/12in	16mm/½in
		13	main	G5/15	7500	525mm/21in	16mm/½in
	compact	7	main	G23	5000		
		9	main	G23	5000		
		11	main	G23	5000		
		18	main	G23	5000		
		24	main	G23	5000		
		35	main	G23	5000		

TUNGSTEN-HALOGEN	DESCRIPTION	WATTAGE	VOLTAGE	CAP	BULB LIFE	BEAM ANGLE
	tubular bulb	100	main	E27	2000	
		150	main	E27	2000	
		250	main	E27	2000	
	multi-mirror bulb	20	12	G × 5.3	3000	7° × 5°
		20	12	G × 5.3	3000	13° × 10°
		20	12	G × 5.3	3000	36° × 37°
		50	12	G × 5.3	3000	13° × 11°
		50	12	G × 5.3	3000	27° × 22°
		50	12	G × 5.3	3000	31° × 37°
		75	12	G × 5.3	3000	15° × 14°
		75	12	G × 5.3	3000	38° × 40°
	metal reflector bulb	50	12	Bal5d	2000	10°
		50	12	Bal5d	2000	30°
	low-voltage reflector bulbs	20	12	G4	2000	10°
		20	12	G4	2000	15°
		35	6	Bal5d	2000	6°
		35	6	Bal5d	2000	14°
		20	12	Bal5d	1000	18° × 32°
	low-voltage bulb	20	12	G4	2000	
		50	12	GY6.35	2000	
		100	12	GY6.35	2000	
		20	24	G4	2000	
		50	24	GY6.35	2000	
		100	24	GY6.35	2000	
	linear bulb	100	main	R7s	1000	
		150	main	R7s	1000	
		200	main	R7s	1000	
		300	main	R7s	1500	
		500	main	R7s	2000	

GLOSSARY

Accent lighting: Used to light details, focus on individual items. Secondary to the overall lighting scheme.

Adapter: Permits more than one plug to be powered by one socket. Be careful not to overload the circuit when using.

Amp (ampere): Unit of electric current.

Backlight: Light projected from behind an object to produce a highlighted silhouette.

Baffle: Attached to light fittings to prevent glare.

Barndoor: Flaps attached to some light fittings to control light, often used to direct light onto an object without lighting the surface.

Batten fitting: Fluorescent fitting with bulb and holder, and control equipment.

Beam angle: Measure of the illumination of a reflector bulb or fitting.

Bi-pin: Two pins of a bulb that insert into the holder to make an electrical connection.

Bounced light or **indirect lighting:** Light reflected off a surface (ie wall or ceiling).

Bulb cap: Electrical connection between the bulb and fitting.

Bulk-head fitting: A sturdy fitting for outdoor and indoor use. Made of metal and glass.

Cold-cathode light: Neon light.

Colour rendition: An object's colour when lit by artificial light, particularly neon or fluorescent light.

Compact fluorescent bulb: Small bulb which works in the same way as a fluorescent tube. Cannot be dimmed.

Cool beam: Bulbs with a beam of light of only 30% of the heat energy of a conventional bulb.

Cross-lighting: Used to accent a detail or object by lighting from two different directions.

Crown-silvered bulb: Tungsten, reflector or incandescent bulb with an internal reflective silver surface. Produces a well-defined beam.

Dichroic: Type of bulb which passes majority of heat backwards, away from the beam of light (eg multi-mirror low-voltage sources).

Diffuser: Scatters the light. Normally part of the light fitting.

Downlighter: Casts light directly downwards, usually mounted or recessed into the ceiling.

Drum uplighter: A low intensity uplighter used for accent lighting.

Eyeball fitting: A downlighter, semi-recessed, with a spherical base that can be swivelled. Light is directed at an angle, like a spotlight.

Filament: Fine metal wire inside a bulb, heated to incandescence by the electric current.

Fluorescent tube: Glass tube filled with an inert gas at low pressure. A coating of fluorescent phosphor powder is agitated by the electric current, emitting light.

Framing projector: Low-voltage fitting with lenses and shutters to shape light beam. Used for accent lighting.

Fuse: Breaks the circuit if there is an electrical fault, preventing fire.

GLS (general lighting service) bulb: Standard incandescent light bulb.

Grolux bulb: Fluorescent bulb with mauve-coloured light. Can be used to grow plants.

Halogen bulb: *See* Tungsten-halogen bulb.

Incandescent bulb: Ordinary domestic light bulb. Current through tungsten filament produces light.

ISL bulb: Reflector bulb, with silver on the interior back surface.

Lamp: Professional name for a light bulb, especially low-voltage.

Load: Total of wattages of all bulbs used in a circuit.

Long life bulb: Bulb which lasts twice as long as ordinary bulb.

Louvre: Baffle of metal or plastic obscuring view of bulb. Often used to turn recessed downlighters into wall-washers.

Low-voltage bulb: A miniature bulb, running on 12 or 24 volts rather than mains voltage. A transformer is used to decrease the voltage.

Lux: Unit used to measure amount of light falling on a surface.

Mercury-vapour bulb: Produces a greenish-blue light. Often used for outdoor lighting.

Metal-halide bulb: Produces a very bright white light. Used for outdoor and commercial lighting.

Neon light: Tube containing neon gas at low pressure. Emits a red light when electricity passes through it.

PAR (parabolic aluminized reflector) bulb: Produces a powerful beam of light by way of an integral reflector. Made of heat-resistant glass.

Reflector: Surface that reflects light produced by a bulb.

Reflector bulb: Any bulb which directs light outwards by way of an internal reflector.

Scoop reflector: Added to wall-washers to spread light to the top of a wall.

Sodium bulb: Bulb containing neon and sodium vapour. Emits an orange light. Used in outdoor lighting, especially floodlights and streetlamps.

Spotlight: Generic term for variety of light sources which produce a direct beam. Used for accent lighting.

Striplight: A tube-shaped bulb with a tungsten filament.

Track: Insulated conductor to which light fittings are clipped. Versions carrying several circuits are available.

Transformer: Reduces the electricity supply from mains voltage to lower voltage. Essential for any low-voltage light fitting.

Tungsten bulb: Incandescent bulb. Contains a tungsten filament.

Tungsten striplight: Incandescent tube-shaped fitting with a tungsten filament.

Tungsten-halogen bulb: Also quartz-halogen bulb, or halogen bulb. Bulb with a tungsten filament containing halogen gas. Gives a brighter light than a tungsten bulb.

Uplighter: A light fitting which illuminates a room by reflecting light off the ceiling. These may be wall or floor-mounted, or freestanding.

Va rating: Measure of the wattage that can be connected to a transformer.

Volt: Unit of electrical potential of a circuit.

Wall-washer: A light fitting, usually ceiling-mounted, which casts an even light down a wall.

Watt: Unit of energy produced by an electrical appliance.

STOCKISTS AND SUPPLIERS

UK

British Home Stores plc, Head Office, Marylebone House, 129 Marylebone Road, London NW1. 0171 262 3288

Concord Lighting Ltd, 174 High Holborn, London EC1V 7AA. 0171 497 1400

John Cullen Lighting Ltd, 216 Fulham Palace Road, London W6 9NT. 0171 381 8944

Heal & Son Ltd, 196 Tottenham Court Road, London W1. 0171 636 1666

Texas Homecare, Homecharm House, Park Farm, Wellingborough, Northants, NN6 3XA. 01933 679679

Christopher Wray's Lighting Emporium, 600 King's Road, London SW6. 0171 736 8434

US

Capitol Lighting & Supply, 200 Locust Street, Hertford, CT 06141. (203) 549 1230

Lightolier, 100 Lighting Way, Secaucus, NJ 07096. (201) 864 3000

R. H. Macy & Co, 1301 Avenue of the Americas, New York, NY 10019. (800) 222 6161

Sears Roebuck, Sears Tower, Chicago, Ill 60684. (800) 366 3000

INDEX